BEGINNING PIANO SOLO   2ND EDITION

Disney Hits

ISBN 978-1-5400-2200-4

Disney Characters and Artwork © Disney

7777 W. BLUEMOUND RD. P.O. BOX 13819 MILWAUKEE, WI 53213

In Australia Contact:
Hal Leonard Australia Pty. Ltd.
4 Lentara Court
Cheltenham, Victoria, 3192 Australia
Email: ausadmin@halleonard.com.au

For all works contained herein:
Unauthorized copying, arranging, adapting, recording, Internet posting, public performance,
or other distribution of the printed music in this publication is an infringement of copyright.
Infringers are liable under the law.

Visit Hal Leonard Online at
www.halleonard.com

CIRCLE OF LIFE
from THE LION KING

Music by ELTON JOHN
Lyrics by TIM RICE

Moderately slow

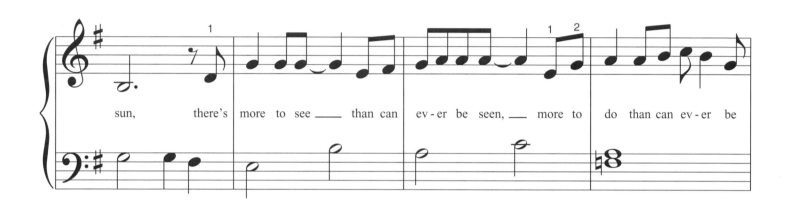

© 1994 Wonderland Music Company, Inc.
All Rights Reserved. Used by Permission.

small on the end - less round. ___ It's the cir - cle of life, and it moves us all _

_ through des - pair and hope, ____ through faith and _

love, 'til we find our place ___ on the path un - wind - ing

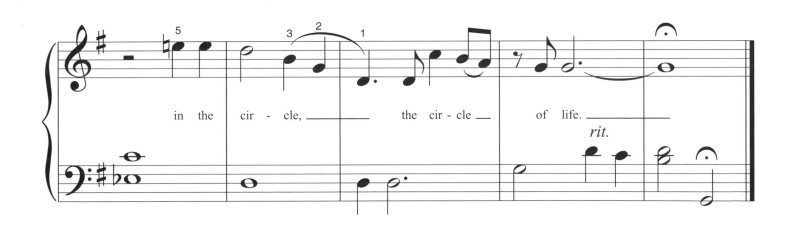

in the cir - cle, ___ the cir - cle _ of life. ___
rit.

EVERMORE
from BEAUTY AND THE BEAST

Music by ALAN MENKEN
Lyrics by TIM RICE

Moderately slow, with freedom

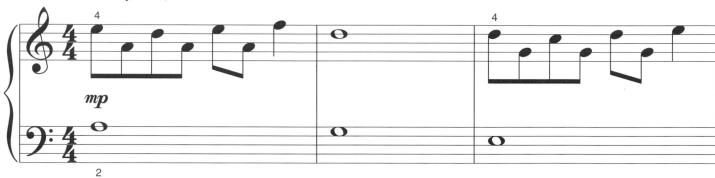

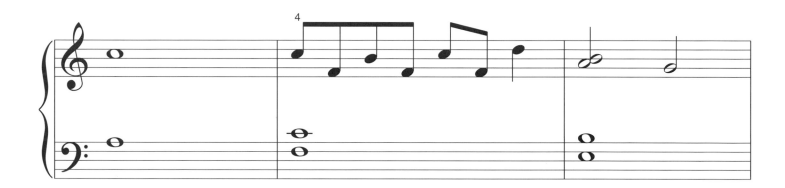

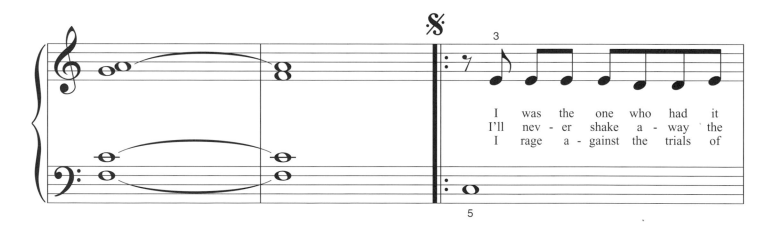

I was the one who had it
I'll nev- er shake a - way the
I rage a - gainst the trials of

all;
pain.
love.

I was the mas- ter of my fate.
I close my eyes, but she's still there.
I curse the fad- ing of the light.

© 2017 Wonderland Music Company, Inc.
All Rights Reserved. Used by Permission.

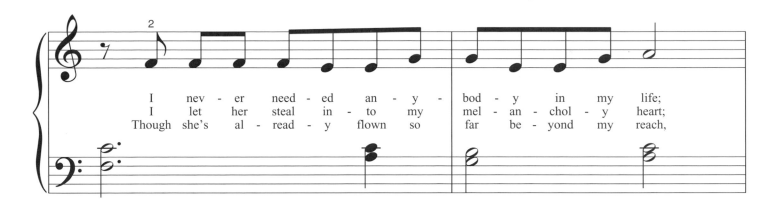

I   nev - er need - ed an - y - bod - y in my life;
I   let her steal in - to my mel - an - chol - y heart;
Though she's al - read - y flown so far be - yond my reach,

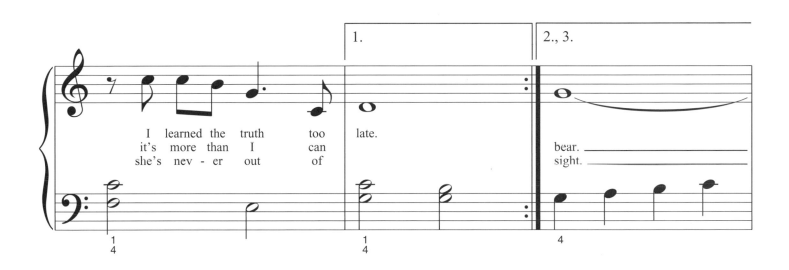

I learned the truth too late.
it's more than I can bear. _____
she's nev - er out of sight. _____

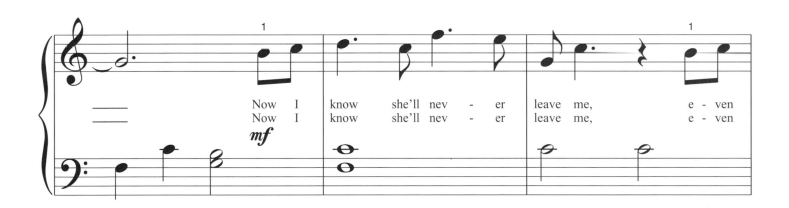

Now I know she'll nev - er leave me, e - ven
Now I know she'll nev - er leave me, e - ven

as she runs a - way. She will still tor - ment _____ me,
as she fades from view. She will still in - spire me,

calm me, hurt ____ me, move me, come what may.
be a part ____ of ev - 'ry - thing I do.

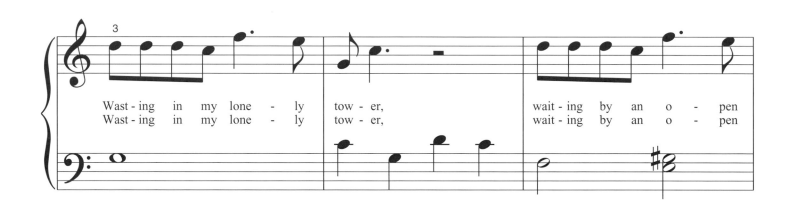

Wast - ing in my lone - ly tow - er, wait - ing by an o - pen
Wast - ing in my lone - ly tow - er, wait - ing by an o - pen

To Coda

door, I'll fool my - self she'll walk right in,
door,

D.S. al Coda
(no repeat)

and be with me for - ev - er more.

CODA

I'll fool my-self she'll walk right in,

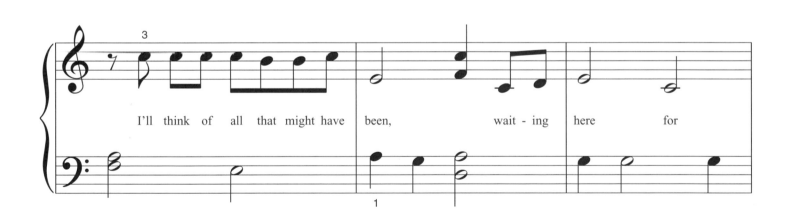

and as the long, long nights be - gin,

I'll think of all that might have been, wait - ing here for

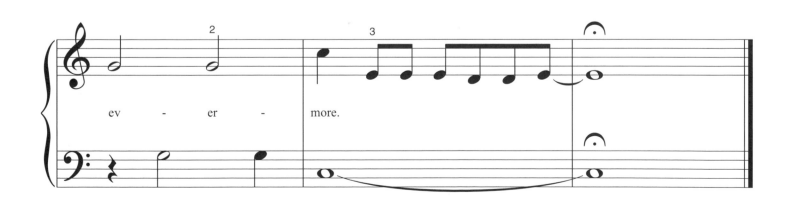

ev - er - more.

HOW DOES A MOMENT LAST FOREVER

from BEAUTY AND THE BEAST

Music by ALAN MENKEN
Lyrics by TIM RICE

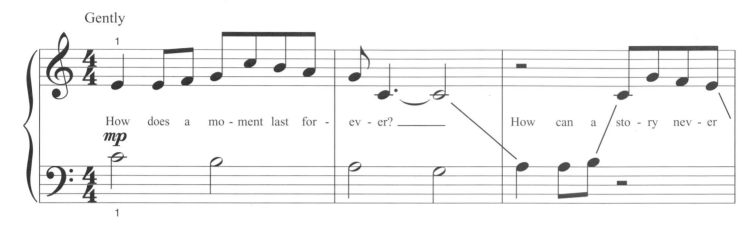

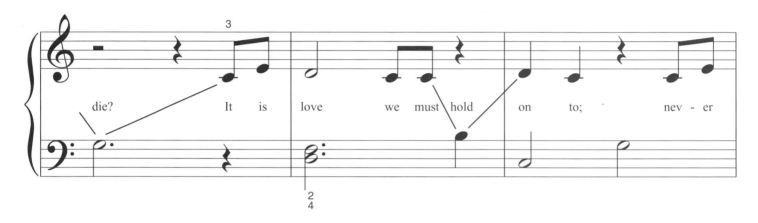

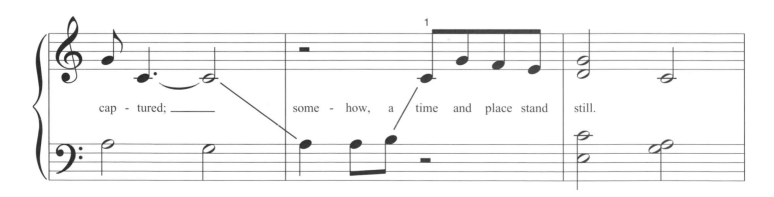

© 2017 Wonderland Music Company, Inc.
All Rights Reserved. Used by Permission.

Love lives on ____ in - side our hearts ____ and al - ways

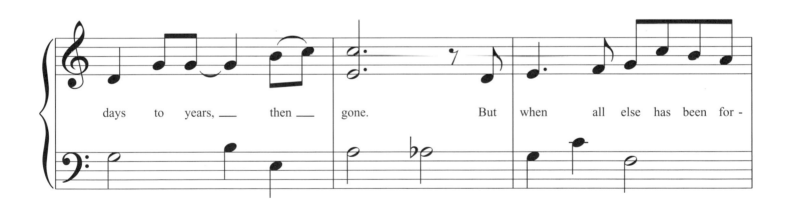

will. Min - utes turn to hours; ____

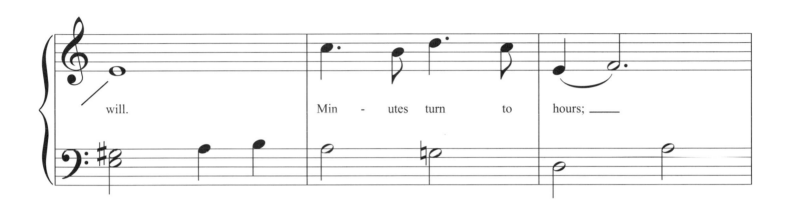

days to years, ____ then ____ gone. But when all else has been for -

got - ten, still our song lives on.

HOW FAR I'LL GO
from MOANA

Music and Lyrics by
LIN-MANUEL MIRANDA

Moderately

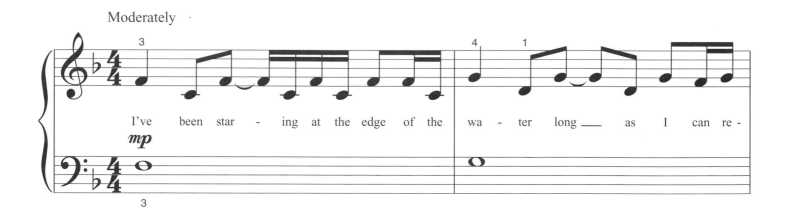

I've been star - ing at the edge of the wa - ter long __ as I can re -

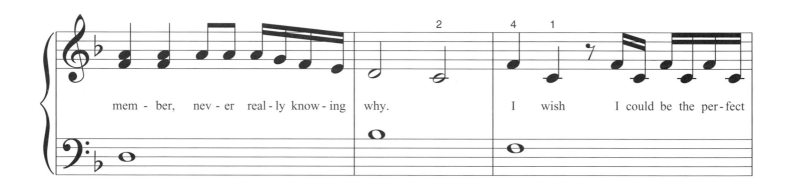

mem - ber, nev - er real - ly know - ing why. I wish I could be the per - fect

daugh - ter, but I come back to the wa - ter no mat - ter how hard I try. Ev - 'ry

turn I take, ev - 'ry trail I track, ev - 'ry path I make, ev - 'ry road leads back to the

© 2016 Walt Disney Music Company
All Rights Reserved. Used by Permission.

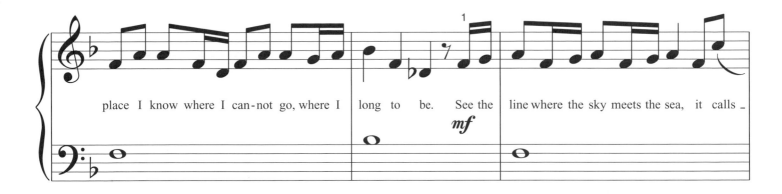

place I know where I can-not go, where I long to be. See the line where the sky meets the sea, it calls

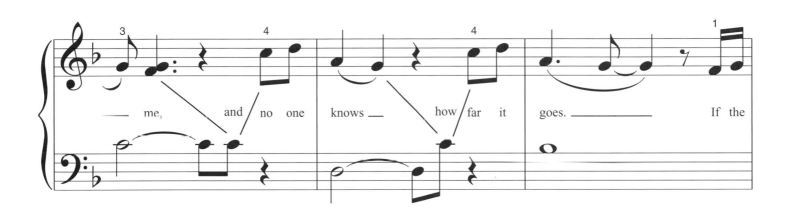

me, and no one knows how far it goes. If the

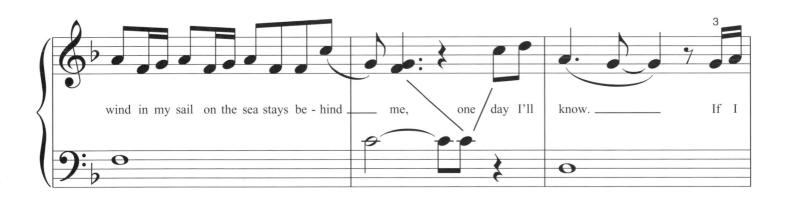

wind in my sail on the sea stays be - hind me, one day I'll know. If I

go, there's just no tell - ing how far I'll go. I know ev - 'ry - bod - y on this

is - land seems __ so hap - py on this is - land. Ev - 'ry - thing is by de - sign. __

__ I know ev - 'ry - bod - y on this is - land has __ a role on this

is - land, so may - be I can roll with mine. __ I can lead with pride, I can make us strong. I'll be

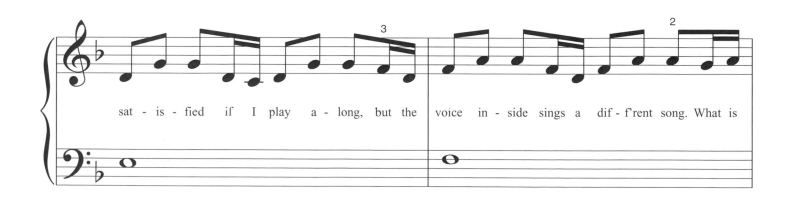

sat - is - fied if I play a - long, but the voice in - side sings a dif - f'rent song. What is

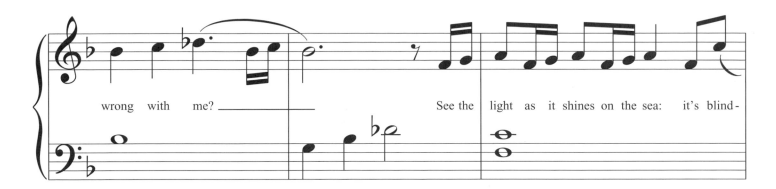

wrong with me? _____ See the light as it shines on the sea: it's blind-

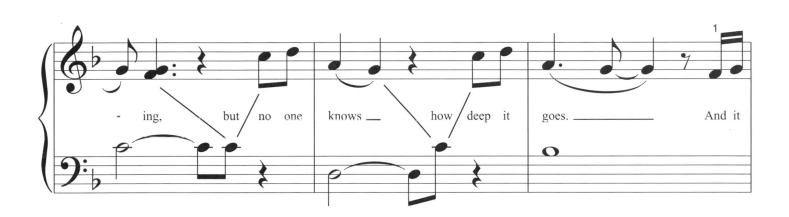

- ing, but no one knows ___ how deep it goes. _____ And it

seems like it's call-ing out to me, so come find ___ me and let me

know. _____ What's be - yond that line? Will I cross that line? The

line where the sky meets the sea, it calls _____ me, and no one knows ___ how far it

goes. _____ If the wind in my sail on the sea stays be - hind _

___ me, one day I'll know _____ how far I'll go. ____

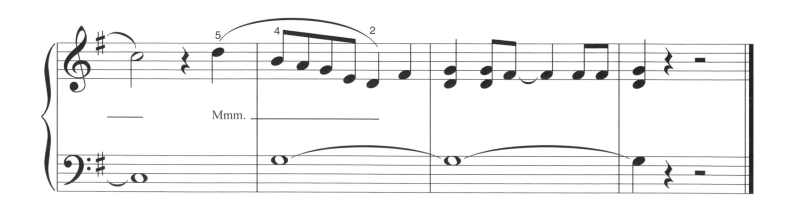

___ Mmm. _____

UNDER THE SEA
from THE LITTLE MERMAID

Music by ALAN MENKEN
Lyrics by HOWARD ASHMAN

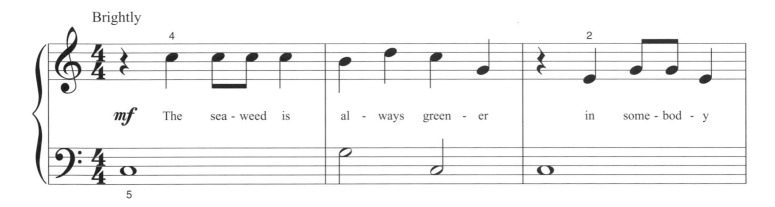

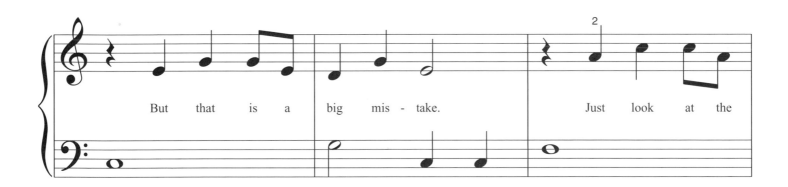

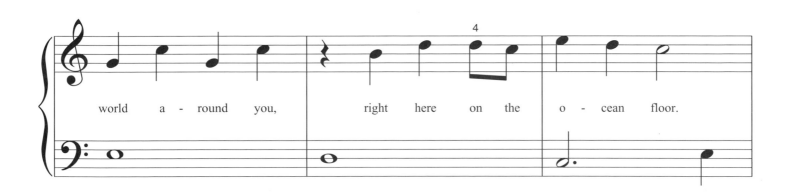

© 1988 Wonderland Music Company, Inc. and Walt Disney Music Company
All Rights Reserved.   Used by Permission.

Such won - der - ful things sur - round you. What more is you

look - in' for? Un - der the sea,

un - der the sea. Dar - lin', it's

bet - ter down where it's wet - ter. Take it from me.

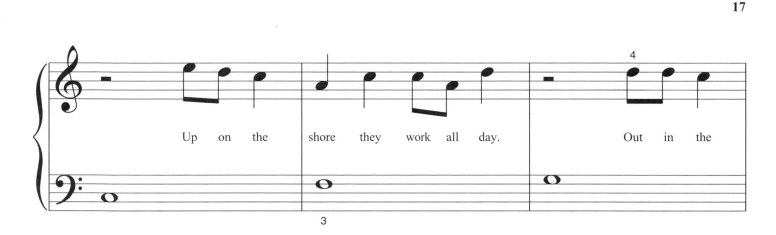

Up on the shore they work all day. Out in the

sun they slave a - way. While we de - vo - tin' full - time to

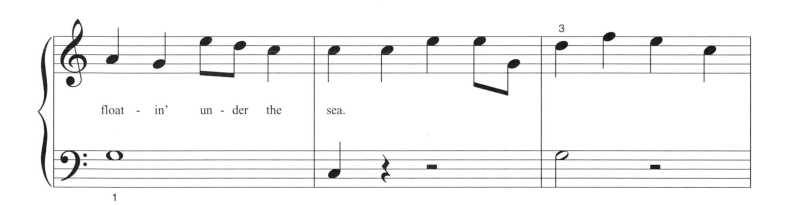

float - in' un - der the sea.

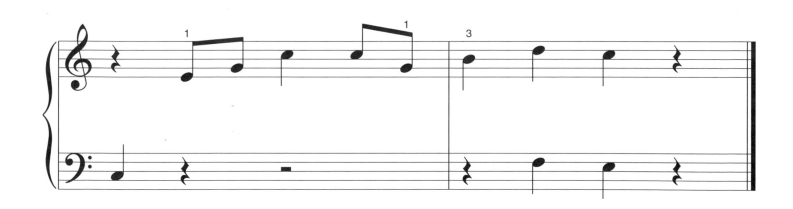

WHEN SHE LOVED ME

from TOY STORY 2

Music and Lyrics by
RANDY NEWMAN

Tenderly

When some-bod-y loved me, ev-'ry-thing was beau-ti-ful.

Ev-'ry hour we spent to-geth-er lives with-in my heart.

And when she was sad, I was there to dry her tears;

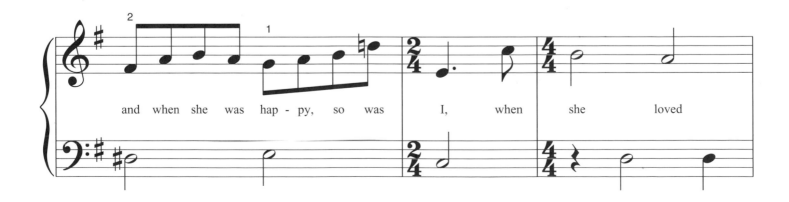

and when she was hap-py, so was I, when she loved

© 1999 Walt Disney Music Company and Pixar Talking Pictures
All Rights Reserved. Used by Permission.

me. Through the sum - mer and the fall, we had each oth - er, that was all. Just

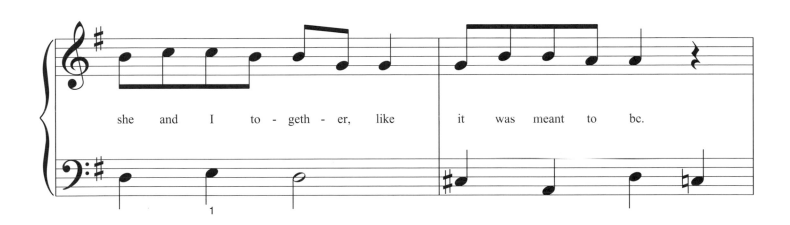

she and I to - geth - er, like it was meant to be.

And when she was lone - ly, I was there to com - fort her, and knew that

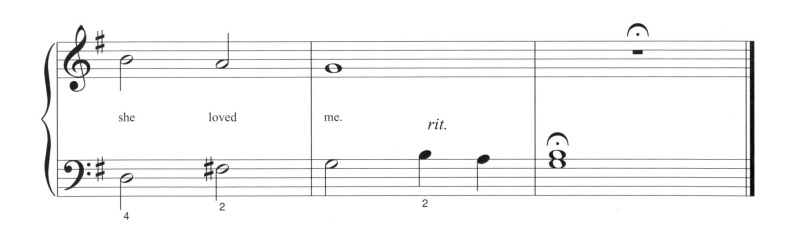

she loved me. *rit.*

A WHOLE NEW WORLD

from ALADDIN

Music by ALAN MENKEN
Lyrics by TIM RICE

Moderately

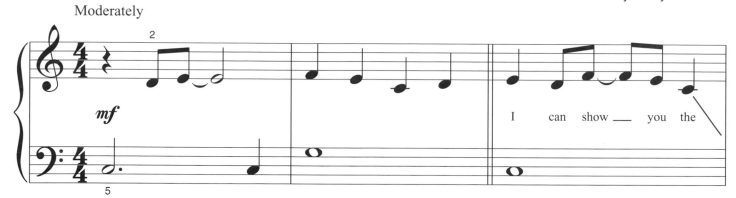

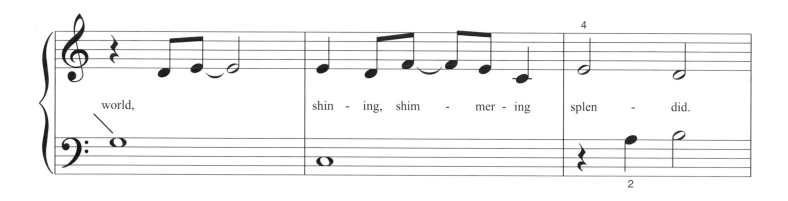

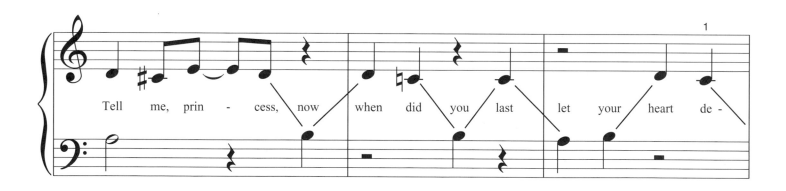

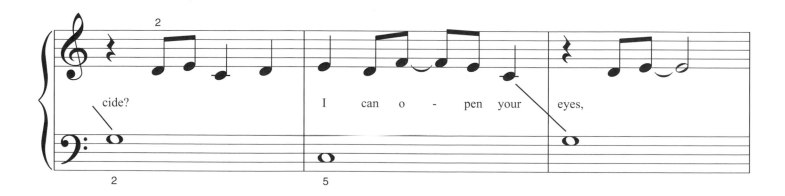

© 1992 Wonderland Music Company, Inc. and Walt Disney Music Company
All Rights Reserved. Used by Permission.

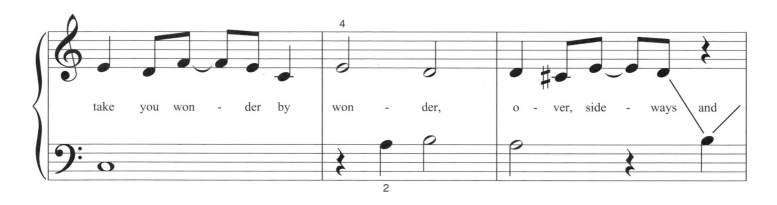

take you won - der by won - der, o - ver, side - ways and

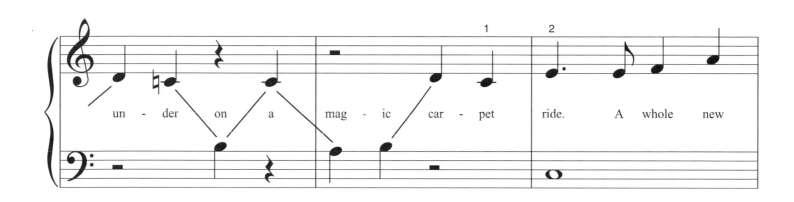

un - der on a mag - ic car - pet ride. A whole new

world, _____ a new fan - tas - tic point of

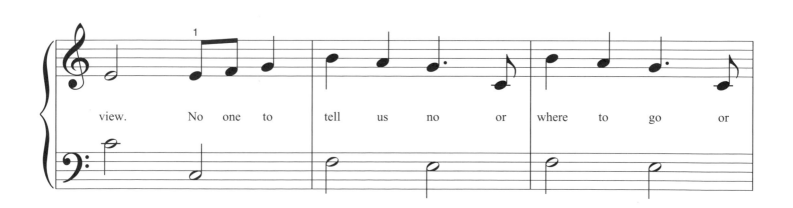

view. No one to tell us no or where to go or

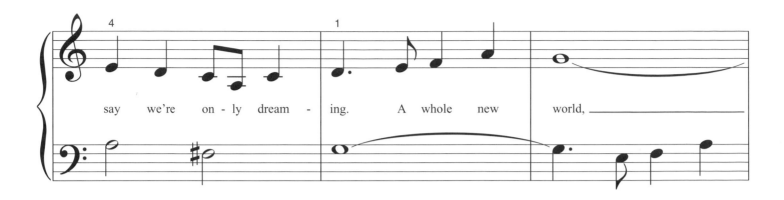

say we're on-ly dream - ing. A whole new world,

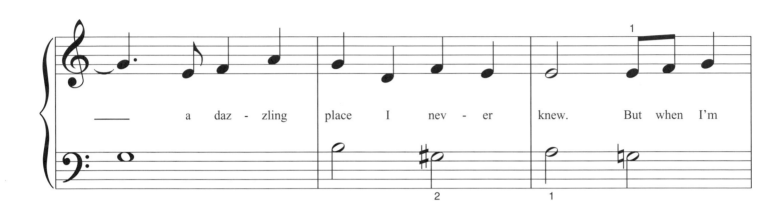

a daz - zling place I nev - er knew. But when I'm

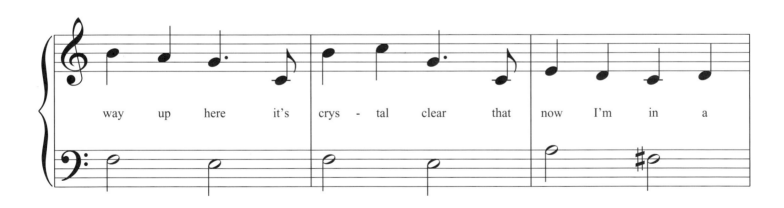

way up here it's crys - tal clear that now I'm in a

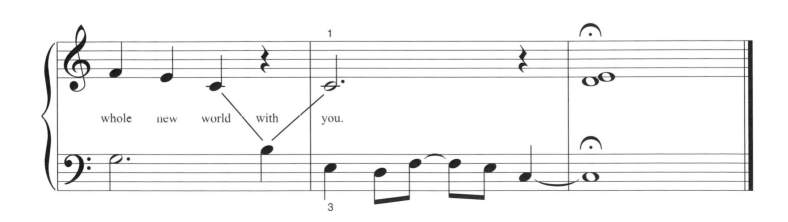

whole new world with you.

YOU'RE WELCOME
from MOANA

Music and Lyrics by
LIN-MANUEL MIRANDA

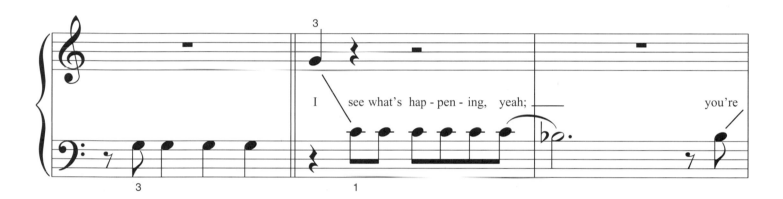

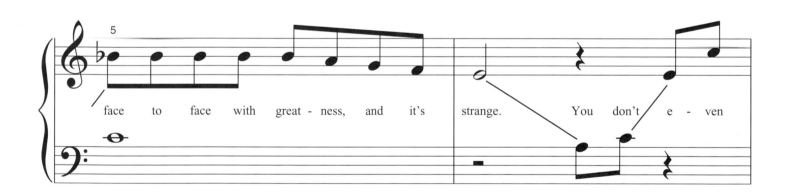

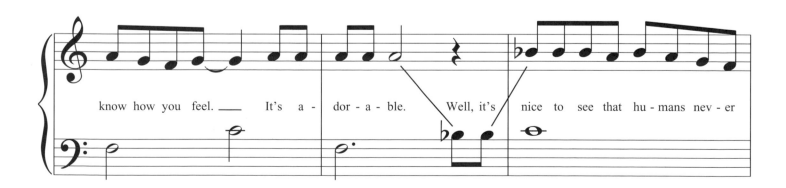

© 2016 Walt Disney Music Company
All Rights Reserved. Used by Permission.

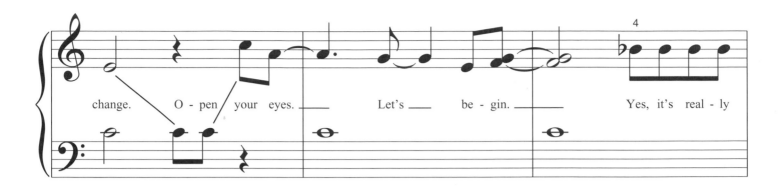

change. O - pen your eyes. ____ Let's ____ be - gin. ____ Yes, it's real - ly

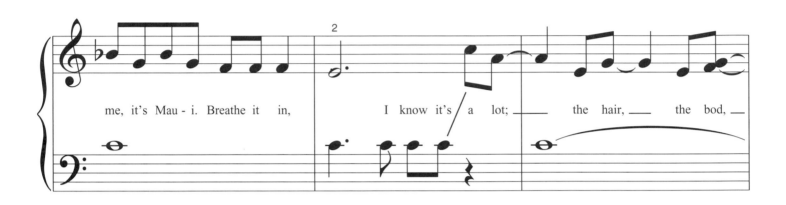

me, it's Mau - i. Breathe it in, I know it's a lot; ____ the hair, ____ the bod, ____

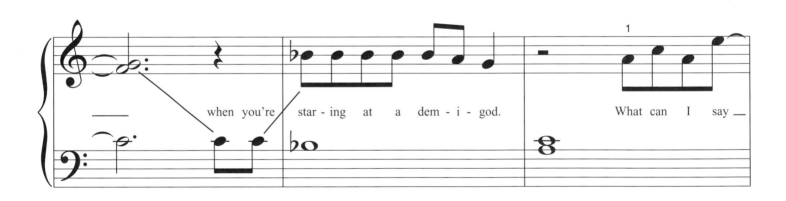

____ when you're star - ing at a dem - i - god. What can I say ____

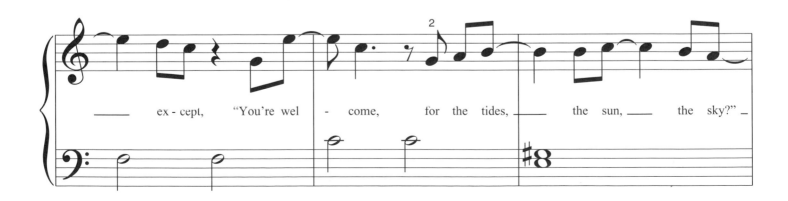

____ ex - cept, "You're wel - come, for the tides, ____ the sun, ____ the sky?" ____

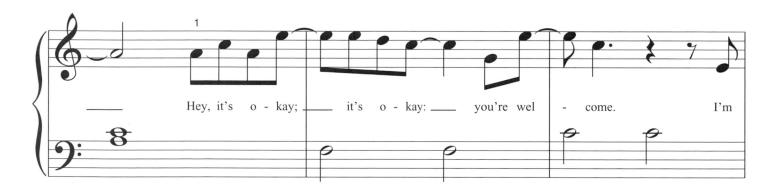

Hey, it's o - kay; it's o - kay: you're wel - come. I'm

just an or - di - nar - y dem - i - guy. Hey, what has two thumbs

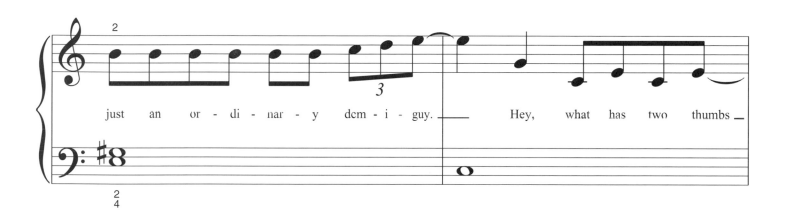

and pulled up the sky when you were wad - dl - ing yea high? This guy!

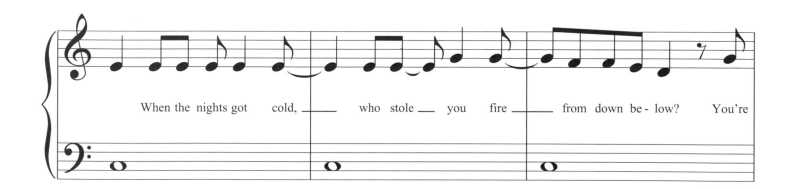

When the nights got cold, who stole you fire from down be - low? You're

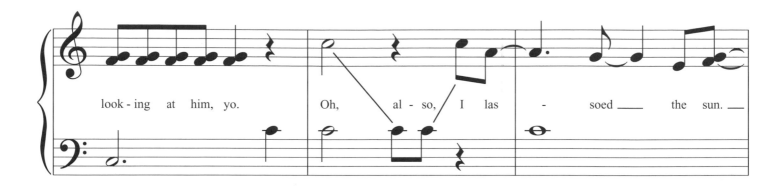

look - ing at him, yo. Oh, al - so, I las - soed _____ the sun. _____

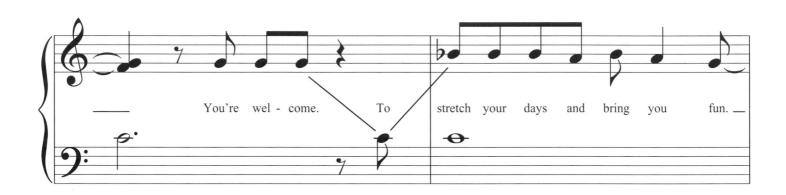

_____ You're wel - come. To stretch your days and bring you fun. _____

_____ Al - so, I har - nessed _____ the breeze. _____ You're wel - come. To

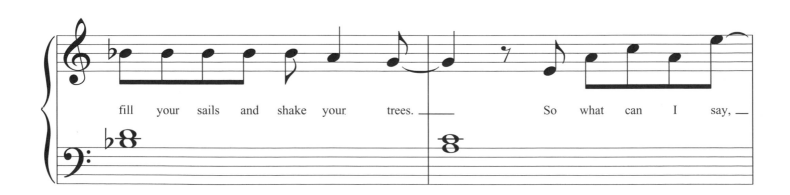

fill your sails and shake your trees. _____ So what can I say, _____

WRITTEN IN THE STARS

from AIDA

Music by ELTON JOHN
Lyrics by TIM RICE

Moderately slow

mf I am here to tell you we can nev-er meet a-gain.
Nev-er won-der what I'll feel as liv-ing shuf-fles by.

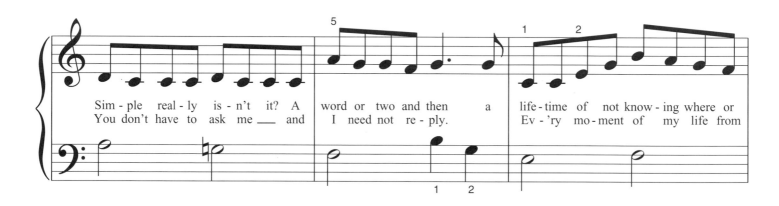

Sim-ple real-ly isn't it? A word or two and then a life-time of not know-ing where or
You don't have to ask me ___ and I need not re-ply. Ev-'ry mo-ment of my life from

how or why or when. You think of me or speak of me and won-der what be-fell the
now un-til I die think or dream of you and fail to un-der-stand how a

some-one you once loved so long a-go ___ so well!
per-fect love can be con-found-ed out of hand. Is it

1.
2.

© 1998 Wonderland Music Company, Inc., Happenstance Ltd. and Evadon Ltd.
All Rights Reserved. Used by Permission.

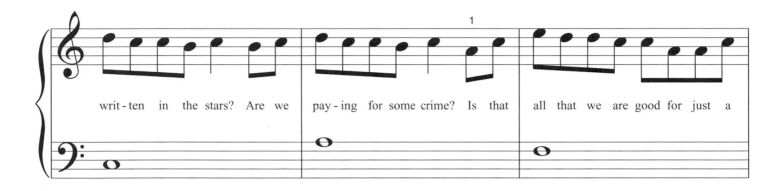

writ-ten in the stars? Are we pay-ing for some crime? Is that all that we are good for just a

stretch of mor-tal time? Or some God's ex-per-i-ment in which we have no say? In

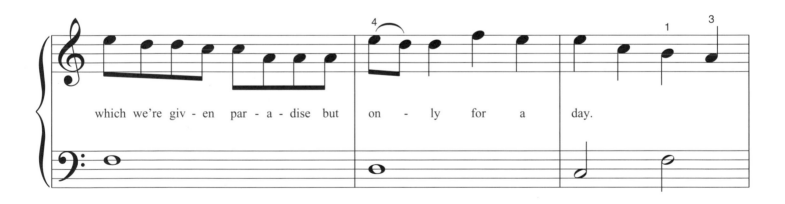

which we're giv-en par-a-dise but on - ly for a day.

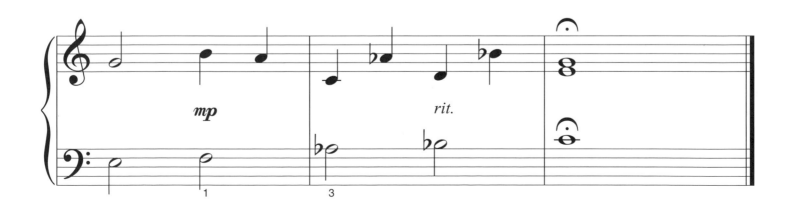

mp　　*rit.*

YOU'VE GOT A FRIEND IN ME

from TOY STORY

Music and Lyrics by
RANDY NEWMAN

© 1995 Walt Disney Music Company
All Rights Reserved. Used by Permission.

you've got a friend in

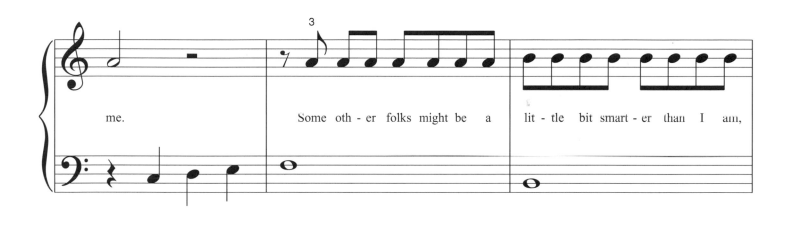

me. Some oth - er folks might be a lit - tle bit smart - er than I am,

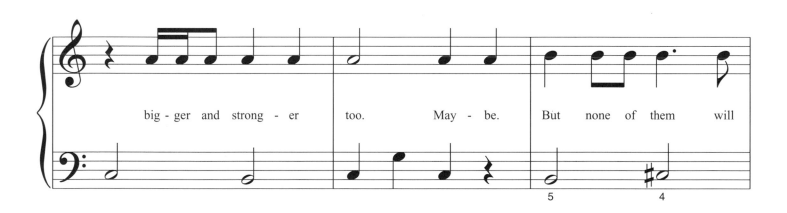

big - ger and strong - er too. May - be. But none of them will

ev - er love you the way I do, just me and you boy. And, as the years go

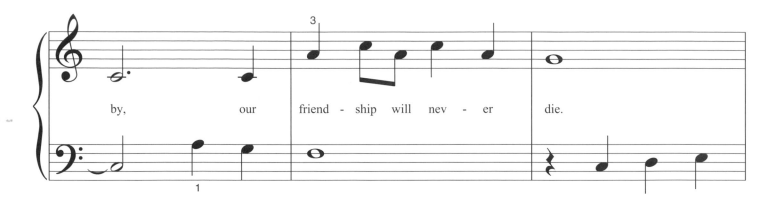

by, our friend - ship will nev - er die.

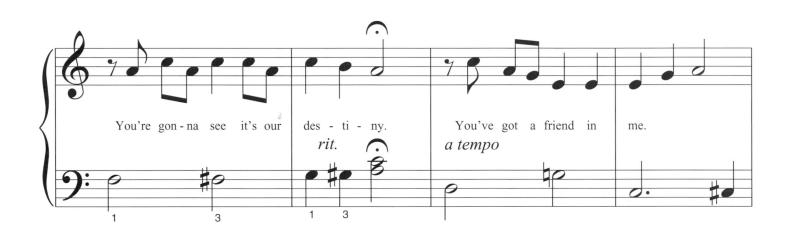

You're gon-na see it's our des - ti - ny. You've got a friend in me.

rit. *a tempo*

You've got a friend in me. You've got a friend in me.

rit.